W9-DIY-251

WEEKLY WR READER®
EARLY LEARNING LIBRARY

How People Lived in America
Clothing in American History

by Dana Meachen Rau

Reading consultant:
Susan Nations, M.Ed.,
author/literacy coach/
consultant in literacy development

Please visit our web site at: www.garethstevens.com
For a free color catalog describing Weekly Reader® Early Learning Library's list
of high-quality books, call 1-877-445-5824 (USA) or 1-800-387-3178 (Canada).
Weekly Reader® Early Learning Library's fax: (414) 336-0164.

Library of Congress Cataloging-in-Publication Data

Rau, Dana Meachen, 1971-
    Clothing in American history / by Dana Meachen Rau.
       p. cm. — (How people lived in America)
    Includes bibliographical references and index.
    ISBN-10: 0-8368-7205-3 — ISBN-13: 978-0-8368-7205-7 (lib. bdg.)
    ISBN-10: 0-8368-7212-6 — ISBN-13: 978-0-8368-7212-5 (softcover)
    1. Clothing and dress—United States—Juvenile literature. 2. Clothing and dress—
United States—History—Juvenile literature. I. Title.
    GT605.R38   2007
    391.00973—dc22   2006008634

This edition first published in 2007 by
Weekly Reader® Early Learning Library
A Member of the WRC Media Family of Companies
330 West Olive Street, Suite 100
Milwaukee, WI 53212 USA

Editor: Barbara Kiely Miller
Art direction: Tammy West
Cover design and page layout: Kami Strunsee
Picture research: Sabrina Crewe

Picture credits: Cover, title page © Alinari Archives/CORBIS; p. 4 © Michael Newman/PhotoEdit;
pp. 6, 7, 9, 13, 14, 15, 16, 17, 18 The Granger Collection, New York; pp. 8, 10, 11 © North Wind
Picture Archives; pp. 12, 19, 20 © Bettmann/CORBIS; p. 21 © Pierre Vauthey/CORBIS SYGMA

Printed in the United States of America

1 2 3 4 5 6 7 8 9 10 09 08 07 06

Table of Contents

Cover: In the late 1800s, children dressed up even when they played.

Today, active children wear clothes that let them move and keep them safe.

What We Wear Today

When children play today, they wear **comfortable** clothes. Long ago, girls and boys dressed in fancy clothes, even when they played outside. Adults dressed differently than they do today, too. Women were not allowed to wear pants. Some men wore white wigs! Clothing has changed a lot over the last four hundred years.

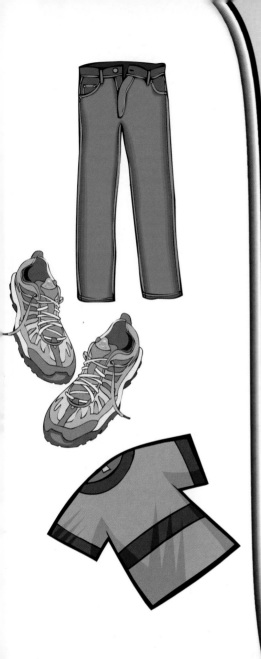

Long ago, people . . .

- did not wear jeans;
- did not wear t-shirts;
- did not wear sneakers;
- did not have clothes with zippers;
- did not buy clothes in a store;
- did not have closets full of clothes.

Women made wool into yarn on a spinning wheel.

Early American Clothing

In the 1600s, most people in America had to make their own clothes. To get cloth, people grew a plant called **flax**. It could be made into a cloth called **linen**. People also raised sheep. They spun the sheep's wool into thread and used it to knit sweaters and **stockings**. People made **leather** from the skins of animals. They used the leather to make shoes.

Until they were about five years old, boys and girls dressed the same. They wore long dresses made of linen or wool. Then, children started dressing like their parents. Boys and men wore linen shirts tucked into **breeches**. Breeches were short pants that only came down to the knees.

This painting of a family shows them dressed in their best clothes.

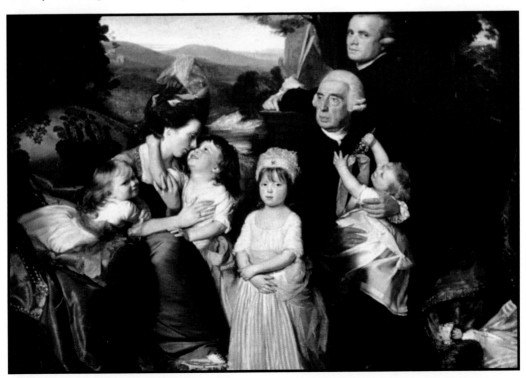

Women wore aprons when they cooked. They wore caps to protect their hair from cooking fires.

Girls and women wore tight tops and long, full skirts. They wore hats called **bonnets** to shade their faces from the sun. Skirts did not have pockets. A woman wore a pocket tied around her waist. An apron kept her skirt from getting dirty while she worked.

Rich people ordered their clothes from Europe. Sailing ships brought the clothes to America. The women wore very fancy dresses. Under the skirt of a fancy dress, a woman wore one or more other skirts. These skirts were called **petticoats**. A woman might carry a fan and wear gloves, too.

When women wore petticoats, their dresses looked big and puffy. The wife of President George Washington wore this kind of dress.

These men are town leaders. Some of them wore wigs with braids.

Rich men wore ruffled shirts. They wore vests, breeches, and coats. Some men wore wigs of curly white hair. Wigs were very heavy. A man wore a wig to show other people that he was a rich or important person.

Mills and Machines

In the early 1800s, people no longer had to make cloth at home. Machines in **mills** now made thread and wove it into cloth. Mills were built next to rivers. The power of the flowing water turned wheels. The wheels ran the mill machines. People bought the mills' cloth to make clothes.

Many young women and girls worked at mills in Massachusetts. They ran the machines that made cloth.

© North Wind Picture Archives

This was the first sewing machine Elias Howe made. It could sew two hundred and fifty stitches a minute.

Some new machines were used in homes. **Sewing** machines were invented in the mid-1800s by Elias Howe and Isaac Singer. Sewing clothes by machine took women less time than sewing them by hand. Starting in the 1860s, women could buy **patterns** for all kinds of clothes that they could make at home.

The Sear's catalog was called "America's Wish Book."

But soon, people no longer had to make all of their own clothes. They could buy clothes that were already made. The first **department store** opened in 1864. It was in Chicago and was named Marshall Fields. People could also order clothes from **catalogs**. If people lived too far from a store, their order was shipped right to their door.

Women stepped into hoops, pulled them up, and tied them at their waists.

Getting Comfortable

During the 1800s, women's clothes were uncomfortable. Women wore **corsets** to make their waists look small. Corsets were so tight that women had trouble breathing. Women also wore big **hoops**, or rings, under their skirts. The hoops made the skirts look wide.

Men who worked in offices dressed to look important. They wore coats and top hats. They used **suspenders** to hold up their pants. Men who worked outdoors needed tougher clothes. In the 1850s, Levi Strauss made jeans out of a strong cloth used to make tents. Farmers, miners, and other men wore Levi jeans to work.

Cowboys wore jeans to work on a ranch. Jeans were blue so they would not show stains.

In the late 1800s, girls and boys played yard games like croquet. They wore fancy clothes even when they were outside.

Children dressed in nice clothes every day. Girls wore dresses that came to their knees. Boys wore **knickers**. These short pants were like the breeches men wore in the past. Both girls and boys wore stockings to cover their legs. Children had to try to keep their clothes clean, even when they played outside.

In the late 1800s and early 1900s, people had more free time to play sports. They wore comfortable clothes to play tennis, golf, and baseball. Sneakers made it easier for people to run. Women still wore dresses to play many of these sports. But to go bicycling, they wore baggy pants called **bloomers**. These were the first pants for women!

Women could move easier and have more fun when they wore pants.

Women who wore short dresses were called "flappers." They rolled down their stockings to show off their knees.

Clothing changed a lot in the 1920s. Women stopped wearing corsets. Their dresses no longer had to reach the floor. Many women wore short skirts. Shorter dresses were easier to move and dance in.

In the 1920s, children stopped dressing like small adults. Clothing makers now made children's clothes that were better to play in. Children could run, jump, and climb trees in play clothes.

Exploring a park was easier for children who wore play clothes.

Women Wear Pants

Between 1914 and 1945, many American men had to leave home to fight in wars. Women took over the men's jobs. Wearing a skirt made some jobs hard to do. Many women started wearing pants. But when the wars ended, most women left those jobs and went back to wearing skirts.

This woman is building an airplane. Wearing pants made her job easier.

In the 1960s, people wanted to have more choices in what they wore. They wanted to be comfortable. Today, people who live in the United States do not dress up all of the time. They wear the clothes that work best for what they plan to do.

In the 1960s, many people wore comfortable and colorful clothes.

Glossary

breeches — tight or loose pants for men and boys that fastened at the knee

catalogs — books or magazines that have pictures and descriptions of things people can order and buy

comfortable — easy to wear

corsets — underwear that was made tighter with laces or hooks to make a woman's waist look smaller

department store — a store that sells all types of items

knickers — loose fitting short pants that gathered just below the knee, worn by men who played sports and by boys

mills — buildings with machines for turning natural materials into items that can be sold

patterns — guides and instructions for making something

petticoats — layers of skirts under a woman's dress

sewing — making or repairing clothing with a needle and thread

stockings — long socks

suspenders — straps worn over the shoulders that hold up pants

For More Information

Books

Children's Clothing of the 1800s. Historic Communities (series). David Schimpky and Bobbie Kalman (Crabtree Publishing)

Clothes in Colonial America. Welcome Books (series). Mark Thomas (Children's Press)

You Forgot Your Skirt, Amelia Bloomer. Shana Corey (Scholastic Press)

Web Site

Dress Up

www.memorialhall.mass.edu/activities/dressup/index.html

From their underwear to their coats, see what children and adults wore in the 1700s, 1800s, and 1900s

Publisher's note to educators and parents: Our editors have carefully reviewed this Web site to ensure that it is suitable for children. Many Web sites change frequently, however, and we cannot guarantee that a site's future contents will continue to meet our high standards of quality and educational value. Be advised that children should be closely supervised whenever they access the Internet.

Index

About the Author

Dana Meachen Rau is the author of more than one hundred and fifty children's books, including nonfiction and books for early readers. She writes about history, science, geography, people, and even toys! She lives with her family in Burlington, Connecticut.